STEPFAMILIES

By
Holly Duhig

BookLife
PUBLISHING

©2018
BookLife Publishing
King's Lynn
Norfolk PE30 4LS

All rights reserved.
Printed in Malaysia.

A catalogue record for this book is
available from the British Library.

ISBN: 978-1-78637-401-1

Written by:
Holly Duhig

Edited by:
Kirsty Holmes

Designed by:
Amy Li

All facts, statistics, web addresses
and URLs in this book were verified
as valid and accurate at time of
writing. No responsibility for any
changes to external websites or
references can be accepted by
either the author or publisher.

PHOTO CREDITS

Front Cover – Monkey Business Images, 2 – adriaticfoto, 4 – DNF Style, szefei, Africa Studio,
5 – Cultura Motion, 6 – Kzenon, 7 – Here, 8 – Ivana P.Nikolic, 9 – HamsterMan, 10 – Iakov
Filimonov, 11 – Oksana Kuzmina, 12 – Ronnachai Palas, 13 – ADS Portrait,
14 – pixelheadphoto digital skillset, 15 – Sannikova Maria, 16 – Rawpixel.com,
17 – Freeograph, 18 – Monkey Business Images, 19 – Africa Studio, 20 – Marcos Mesa Sam
Wordley, 21 – YAKOBCHUK VIACHESLAV,
22 – Kzenon, 23 – MIA Studio

Images are courtesy of Shutterstock.com.
With thanks to Getty Images, Thinkstock Photo and iStockphoto.

STEPFAMILIES

Words that look like **this** can be found in the glossary on page 24.

Changing Families

All families are different and no two are the same. Families change all the time. Change can be scary at first, but it is often a good thing.

You might have two parents or just one. Sometimes parents meet new people and fall in love. These people might become our stepparents.

What Is a Stepparent?

A stepparent is the partner of your mother or father rather than your **biological parent**. Stepparents usually live with you and your other parent.

Father

Stepmum

Daughter

Nate – aged 6

"My stepdad has been around ever since I can remember, so I just call him Dad. My older sister calls him Steve."

You might have had a stepparent for a very long time, or they might have only just joined your family.

7

Stepfamilies

Sometimes stepparents have parents and children of their own. This means you can have stepbrothers, stepsisters and even step-grandparents.

"When my stepdad came to live with us I also got two new brothers. Now we have double the amount of video games!"

Connor – aged 7

The people in your family make up your **family tree**.
When you get a stepparent, your family tree grows new branches.

Dad

Stepmum

Daughter

Mum

Stepbrother

Talking About Your Feelings

If your stepparent is only just joining your family, it might feel like a big change. You might feel worried or upset. It is important to talk about these feelings.

"I was worried my stepdad would take Mum away from me. I told her how I felt and they promised that would never happen."

Nikita – aged 6

Counsellor

You can talk about how you feel to a parent, teacher or even a **family counsellor**. Some counsellors are trained to help families who are going through a change.

You Might Feel Worried

Some children worry that their stepparent will **replace** their other parent. However, stepparents don't want to replace anybody. They just want to be another person who takes care of you.

Remember, meeting a whole new family will be scary for your stepparent too.

You might feel worried about spending time with a new stepmum or stepdad. You might feel like you are leaving your other mum or dad behind. This is not the case.

Getting to know your stepparent doesn't mean you love your other parents any less.

You Might Feel Jealous

Before your stepparent joined your family, you and your mum or dad might have spent a lot of time together. You might not want someone else to join in.

"My stepsister told me she'd never had a mum, so I said she could share mine."

Hannah – aged 7

You might also feel jealous if you have new stepsiblings. You might feel like you have to share your parent. Remember, they probably feel the same way.

You Might Feel Sad

When your family is changing, it might make you miss how things used to be. This can make you feel sad.

Alesha – aged 8

"My mum and dad are **divorced**. Sometimes I miss how our family used to be, but now I have two families who love me very much."

If you are feeling upset, it is important that you tell someone. If you talk to your mum or dad they will be able to answer any questions that you might have.

Family Arguments

Because stepparents want to look after you, they might sometimes tell you what to do. This might take some getting used to.

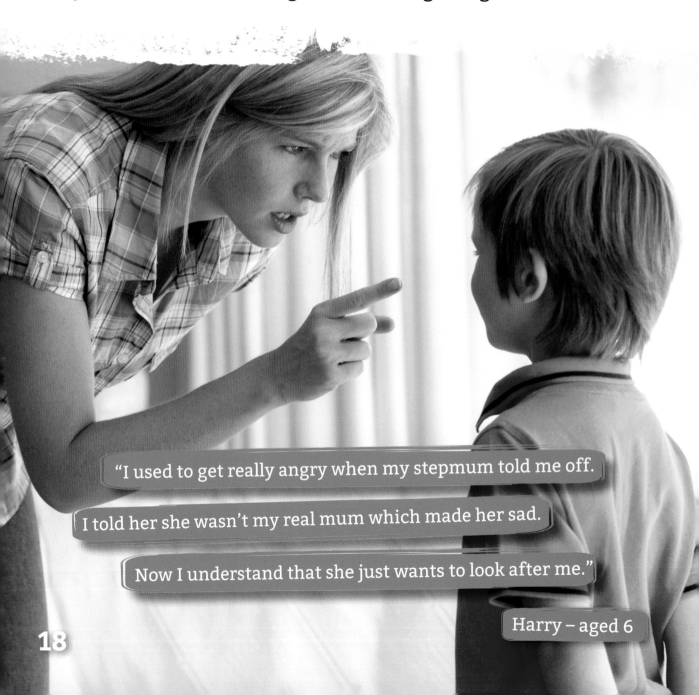

"I used to get really angry when my stepmum told me off.

I told her she wasn't my real mum which made her sad.

Now I understand that she just wants to look after me."

Harry – aged 6

18

It can be hard to share a parent, but there's always more than enough love to go around!

Like all siblings, stepsiblings sometimes argue. You and your stepsiblings might feel **protective** over your things. Learning to share is something all brothers and sisters have to do.

19

Family Fun

There might be arguments sometimes, but there will be lots of fun too. Days out can be even more fun with new people.

Daniel – aged 7

"My mum doesn't like football, but Paul, my new stepdad does! He takes me to matches on Sundays."

The great thing about stepparents is that they have chosen to be your parent and to spend time with you.

Having a stepfamily just means having more people who love you.

New Beginnings

Your stepparent joined your family because they fell in love with your mum or your dad. Because of this, they might decide to get married.

Abigail – aged 8

"When my dad married my stepmum, I got to be a bridesmaid. I felt lucky because lots of children don't get to see their parents get married."

Change can be worrying at first,

but it can be a good thing!

Sometimes parents and stepparents might decide to have a baby. This means you'll have a new brother or sister and your family will grow even more.

23

GLOSSARY

biological parent	the woman who gave birth to a child or the man who is related by birth to a child
divorced	once married but now legally separated
family counsellor	a person whose job it is to listen and give advice to families
family tree	a diagram that shows the relationships between people in a family
protective	having a strong wish to protect someone or something
replace	to take the place of

INDEX